Great

ENTREPRENEUR

in Training

Great Entrepreneur in Training

A Step-by-Step Guide to Navigating and Enhancing Your Entrepreneurship with Practical Exercises and Insights

KEMONE S-G BROWN-TSHABALALA

Published by Tamarind Hill Press in 2023

Although I am a business coach, I am not your coach/mentor. Using this book does not create a mentorship/coaching relationship between us. It is also not intended to be a source of financial or legal advice. Making adjustments to a financial strategy or plan should only be undertaken after consulting with a professional. The publisher and the author make no guarantee of financial results obtained by using this book.

First published in Great Brittain by

Tamarind Hill Press

G33 Evans Incubation Centre, Durham Way South, Newton Aycliffe Business Park, County Durham, DL5 6XP

www.tamarindhillpress.com

Tamarind Hill Press Limited Reg. No. 14023099

A CIP catalogue record for this book is available from the British Library.

PRINT ISBN: 978-1-915161-49-9

TAMARiND HiLL
.PRESS

Contents

Introduction.. 6

Understanding Entrepreneurship................................... 8

Is Entrepreneurship Right for You?................................13

Planting the Seed 17

    Self-Assessment Questionnaire................................. 18

Nurturing Growth..26

    Self-Reflection Exercise: Discovering Your Entrepreneurial Drive
    and Values.. 27

    Defining Your Business Identity: Vision Board and Mind Map 42

Branching Out 51

    Strengths and Weaknesses Assessment........................ 52

    Goal Setting and Action Planning: Turning Dreams into Reality.... 63

Bearing Fruit 70

    Financial Health Check 71

    Market Research and Customer Persona Development: Navigating
    Your Target Audience 82

    Marketing and Branding Strategy 93

    Networking and Relationship Building: Expanding Your Circle of
    Influence... 100

    Time Management and Productivity: Mastering Your Daily Tasks
    107

Reflect and Grow 120

    Mentorship and Support Network 120

    Self-Assessment Questionnaire.................................. 128

    Additional Notes.. 135

    Put it in Your Back Pocket 146

      Accounting Terms Every Entrepreneur Must Know 146

Introduction

"I always knew I was a winner, and I just kept visualizing myself winning."

– Serena Williams

I could not consider the **Great Entrepreneurs … Are Found on the Other Side of the Pressure** book complete without offering you some practical assistance on your entrepreneurial journey. Beyond being empowered through the stories shared by the women in the book, I wanted you to be able to get straight to work on your own businesses, whether it is still just an idea or an already established business facing its own challenges. To this end, I have curated this thoughtfully crafted workbook to empower you as an entrepreneur. The information and activities are your keys to self-discovery, growth, and transformation on your own entrepreneurial journey.

As a business coach and mentor, I understand the importance of self-awareness, goal setting, and continuous improvement on the path to success in business. In the same breath, I know from experience that it takes knowing oneself, being open to growth, and more than anything, being honest about your capabilities. Anyone can develop any skillset, and when it comes to entrepreneurship, it is important to know what it entails so you can decide whether it is right for you. These exercises will guide you through a comprehensive journey of introspection, strategizing, and skill-building. They will help you harness your strengths, identify opportunities, and overcome challenges.

It is not a race, so do not rush the process. Take your time with each exercise, and remember that self-reflection and self-improvement are ongoing processes. Your entrepreneurial drive and values, business identity, strengths and weaknesses, goals, financial health, customer understanding, marketing strategy, relationships, time management, and support network are all critical elements of your journey. It will take you some time to assess each extensively. Try not to do it in one sitting and overwhelm yourself. This alone can affect your ability to walk away from the workbook with valuable lessons and strategies to move your business forward and we do not, by any means, want that.

Now, as you complete the exercises that I have prepared for you, keep an open mind, stay committed, and be ready to discover new insights about yourself and your business. Your entrepreneurial potential is waiting to be unlocked, and your dreams are within reach. Remember, your own limitation is you; so refuse to limit yourself.

For some of the exercises in this workbook, there is writing space for you to record your responses. You do not need to use all the space. It's not a requirement of completing any of the exercises. However, if you need more space to keep writing a response, turn to the back of the book to find extra pages to continue on.

Let's dive in and unleash your full entrepreneurial potential.

Understanding Entrepreneurship

When we hear the term "entrepreneurship," we often think of popular, bold risk-takers, well-known visionary leaders, and the creators of some of the world's most iconic companies. Rarely do we think about the woman on the side of the road selling fruits to make a living or the man who walks around our neighbourhood trying to convince us to let him be our go-to landscaper. Yes, these are often entrepreneurs engaged in entrepreneurship. Why then do we not make the connection? What exactly is entrepreneurship, and what sets entrepreneurs apart from the rest of the business world?

Entrepreneurship, at its core, is the process of identifying opportunities, creating value, and taking calculated risks to bring *innovative* ideas to life. The first note that I want you to take from this definition is that it didn't say anything about going big. Entrepreneurship is not reserved for 'rich people' and one doesn't need to have a business on the high street to be an entrepreneur. Secondly, note the word innovative is in italics. Another term that we often confuse. Innovation does not mean that someone has to come up with an idea that no one has thought or heard of before. In essence, you can sell the exact same product as everyone else but do it in a completely different [innovative] way that makes your business stand out.

To put things into perspective, let's consider the key elements of entrepreneurship:

1. **Identifying Opportunities:** Entrepreneurs possess a keen ability to spot gaps in the market or areas where improvements can be made. They are often driven by a desire to solve problems or meet unmet needs.

2. **Creating Value:** Entrepreneurship is not just about making money; it's about creating value for customers, society, and oneself. Entrepreneurs strive to offer products and/or services that enhance people's lives.

3. **Calculated Risks:** While entrepreneurship involves risk-taking, and a lot of it, it's not reckless. Entrepreneurs assess and mitigate risks to make informed decisions. They are willing to step out of their comfort zones but do so with careful planning.

4. **Innovation:** Innovation is the lifeblood of entrepreneurship. Entrepreneurs introduce novel ideas, methods, or solutions that disrupt existing paradigms and drive progress.

5. **Action-Oriented:** Entrepreneurs are not passive observers; they are doers. They take action to turn their ideas into tangible outcomes.

Now, there is what I call the Entrepreneurial Mindset. I do not believe that everyone readily has the right mindset to be an entrepreneur; though, we can all develop it if we want to. Characteristics can be built, and in time, we will find ourselves ready to take on the task of being entrepreneurs. Understanding what it takes to be an entrepreneur is the first step in that process.

One of the defining characteristics of entrepreneurs is their comfort with uncertainty. Traditional career paths often provide a sense of security and stability, but entrepreneurship is inherently volatile. Entrepreneurs face a myriad of unknowns, from market dynamics to competitive pressures. However, instead of being deterred by uncertainty, they embrace it as an opportunity for growth and innovation, a source of valuable learning experiences. Each challenge or setback presents them a chance to gain insights and adapt their strategies. While comfortable with uncertainty, entrepreneurs are not reckless. They take calculated risks by conducting thorough research, gathering data, and making informed decisions.

Another trait of entrepreneurs is that they are guided by a strong sense of vision and passion for their pursuits. They have a clear picture of what they want to achieve and the impact they wish to make. This vision often serves as their 'why,' providing them with the drive they need to push through the challenges and uncertainties they encounter along the way. Entrepreneurs set ambitious, long-term goals that extend beyond immediate financial gain. Their visions encompass the broader impact of what they've set out to do. This same vision provides resilience, allowing them to weather setbacks and failures because they remain focused on their ultimate objectives.

When it comes to problem solving, entrepreneurs are naturals or have truly honed this skill over time. They view obstacles as puzzles to be solved rather than undefeatable barriers that they can't overcome. This problem-solving mindset drives them to seek innovative solutions and turn challenges into opportunities. Entrepreneurs are adept at identifying pain points and unmet needs in the market. They see problems as opportunities to provide value. Rather than relying on conventional solutions, entrepreneurs think creatively. They explore new approaches, technologies, and business models. Thus, entrepreneurial problem solving is often iterative.

Entrepreneurs must continuously pivot, adjust, and evolve their strategies; consequently, they must be adaptable. They understand that rigid adherence to a single plan can lead to stagnation or failure. They are open to new information and willing to adjust their course of action. Understanding the value of feedback, entrepreneurs actively seek it out from customers, mentors, and advisors. They use this feedback to adapt and improve their products and/or services.

Driven by a bias toward action, entrepreneurs don't linger in the planning phase indefinitely; instead, they take decisive steps to realise their ideas. This action-oriented approach propels them forward. They take the initiative to start projects, make decisions, and implement plans. They don't wait for perfect conditions or guaranteed success. Entrepreneurs understand that the first iteration of a product or strategy may not be perfect. They are willing to make improvements based on real-world feedback. Learning through experience is a fundamental principle of entrepreneurship. Entrepreneurs recognize that practical, hands-on learning is often the most effective.

Now, as we explore the entrepreneurial mindset and what it means to be an entrepreneur, it's important to dispel some common myths about entrepreneurship. These misconceptions can discourage you from becoming an entrepreneur or lead you astray. Let's examine what I consider the most common myths and provide a more accurate picture of entrepreneurship:

Myth #1: Entrepreneurs Are Born, Not Made

Reality: While some individuals may have a natural inclination for entrepreneurship, it is a skill that can be developed and honed. Entrepreneurship education, mentorship, and experience can all contribute to nurturing entrepreneurial abilities.

Myth #2: Entrepreneurs Take Risks, PERIOD!

Reality: Entrepreneurs are not reckless risk-takers; they are calculated risk-takers. They assess risks, mitigate them, and make informed decisions. Entrepreneurship is about managing and navigating risk, not blindly embracing it.

Myth #3: You Need a Revolutionary Idea

Reality: While revolutionary ideas can certainly lead to success, many successful entrepreneurs build on existing concepts and improve upon them. It's often the execution, not just the idea, that matters most.

Myth #4: Entrepreneurship Guarantees Wealth

Reality: Entrepreneurship can be financially rewarding, but it is not a guarantee of wealth. Many entrepreneurs face financial challenges and setbacks throughout the life of their business.

Myths out of the way, how do you go about cultivating that entrepreneurial mindset that I am talking about? The entrepreneurial mindset is not fixed; it can be cultivated and strengthened over time. Whether you're considering entrepreneurship as a new career path or looking to enhance your entrepreneurial abilities, here are some strategies for developing and nurturing this mindset:

1. Embrace Lifelong Learning

Entrepreneurship is a journey of continuous learning. Stay curious and seek knowledge in various domains, from business and technology to psychology and leadership. Read books, take courses, attend seminars, and learn from experienced entrepreneurs.

2. Surround Yourself with the Right People

Build a network of mentors, advisors, and peers who can provide guidance, support, and constructive feedback. Surrounding yourself with like-minded individuals who share your passion for entrepreneurship can be invaluable.

3. Take Calculated Risks

Don't take risks without assessing their potential outcomes. Develop contingency plans and make informed decisions based on research and analysis.

4. Embrace Failure as a Learning Opportunity

Failure is a natural part of entrepreneurship. You are going to fail in one way or another along this journey. Instead of viewing it as a setback, consider it a valuable learning opportunity. Analyse what went wrong, adapt your approach, and apply the lessons learned moving forward.

5. Stay Passionate and Vision-Driven

Maintain a strong sense of passion for your work and a clear vision of your goals. Your passion will fuel your determination, and your vision will provide direction and purpose.

6. Take Action

Remember that entrepreneurship is about doing, not just thinking or planning. Take action, even if it's a small step, and build momentum toward your goals. Learning through practical experience is a crucial aspect of the entrepreneurial journey.

7. Seek Opportunities in Challenges

You are going to face many challenges. The power lies in not letting them get the best of you. Find solutions and turn those problems into your stepping stones.

Ultimately, entrepreneurship is more than a career choice; it's a mindset and a way of approaching the world. It's about seeing opportunities where others see obstacles, embracing uncertainty as a source of growth, and being driven by a passion to create something meaningful.

Is Entrepreneurship Right for You?

In the previous chapter, we explored what entrepreneurship really means and the entrepreneurial mindset. Now, if you are still wondering whether entrepreneurship is the right path for you, this chapter will be of help. We'll now delve into critical aspects of this self-assessment process. This chapter is focussed on answering the why of entrepreneurship. Why do people become entrepreneurs, and is it right for you?

It is important to understand your motivation before embarking on the entrepreneurial journey. Understanding why you want to become an entrepreneur will help you align your goals and aspirations with the challenges and rewards of entrepreneurship. Later, in an exercise, you will work on understanding your own why if you don't already know it. In the meantime, let's look at some of the common motivations for entrepreneurship:

1. **Autonomy:** Many aspiring entrepreneurs are drawn to the idea of being their own boss and having control over their professional lives.
2. **Passion:** A deep passion for a particular product, service, or cause often drives individuals to start businesses that align with their interests.
3. **Innovation:** If you have innovative ideas that can address problems or improve existing solutions, entrepreneurship provides a platform for bringing those ideas to life.
4. **Impact:** Some entrepreneurs are motivated by the desire to make a positive impact on society, whether through social entrepreneurship, environmental initiatives, or community development.
5. **Financial Independence:** Entrepreneurship can offer the potential for financial rewards and wealth creation, but it often requires a significant investment of time and effort in return.

6. **Personal Growth:** The journey of entrepreneurship is a personal growth experience. It challenges individuals to develop new skills, overcome obstacles, and expand their horizons.

Once you've identified your motivations, consider how they align with your entrepreneurial goals. For example, if your motivation is to make a positive impact, you may lean towards social entrepreneurship or businesses with strong corporate social responsibility (CSR) initiatives. If you're driven by financial independence, you'll need to strategize for profitability and sustainable growth.

Entrepreneurship is often romanticized as the pursuit of fearless risk-takers. While entrepreneurs do take risks, the portrayal of a fearless entrepreneur is a myth. In reality, entrepreneurs have varying levels of risk tolerance, and they develop resilience to cope with setbacks and uncertainties. Consider this as the risk-tolerance spectrum:

- **High Risk Tolerance:** Some individuals thrive on high-risk ventures, embracing uncertainty and the potential for significant rewards. They are willing to invest time and resources in ventures with no guaranteed outcomes.
- **Moderate Risk Tolerance:** Many entrepreneurs fall into this category. They take calculated risks, conduct thorough research, and develop contingency plans. While they embrace risk, they aim to manage and mitigate it.
- **Low Risk Tolerance:** Individuals with a low risk tolerance may struggle with the uncertainties of entrepreneurship. They prefer stability and predictability and may find entrepreneurship challenging.

Understanding your risk tolerance is essential for making informed decisions about entrepreneurship. It helps you determine the level of risk you're comfortable with and the strategies you'll employ to manage it. Here are some steps to take to assess your own risk-tolerance level:

1. **Self-Reflection:** Consider your past experiences with risk-taking and how you reacted to uncertain situations.
2. **Financial Assessment:** Evaluate your financial stability and the resources you can allocate to your entrepreneurial venture without jeopardizing your financial well-being.

3. **Scenario Analysis:** Imagine potential worst-case scenarios in your entrepreneurial journey. How would you react, and what steps would you take to mitigate risks?

It's crucial for entrepreneurs to be resilient and passionate as they will face challenges on their journey. However, while passion is essential, it's also important to balance it with realism. Passion alone cannot guarantee success; it needs to be coupled with careful planning, market research, and sound business strategies. Ensure that your passion aligns with a viable business concept.

As you contemplate the path of entrepreneurship, understand that entrepreneurship is not a one-size-fits-all journey; it requires self-awareness and alignment with *your* goals, values, and abilities. Successful entrepreneurs possess a diverse range of skills that empower them to navigate the challenges and complexities of business ownership. While every entrepreneurial journey is unique, certain key skills consistently emerge as critical for success. This workbook will help you in the process of building them. They include:

1. **Creativity:** Entrepreneurship often involves finding innovative solutions to problems and identifying new opportunities. Creative thinking allows entrepreneurs to stand out and differentiate their businesses.
2. **Leadership:** Effective leadership is essential for guiding a team, making tough decisions, and inspiring others to work towards a common goal.
3. **Communication:** Entrepreneurs must communicate their ideas, vision, and goals clearly to team members, investors, and customers. Strong communication skills build trust and credibility.
4. **Adaptability:** The ability to pivot, adjust strategies, and embrace change is vital in the dynamic world of entrepreneurship. Entrepreneurs must remain flexible in response to shifting market conditions.
5. **Financial Literacy:** Understanding financial concepts, budgeting, and financial forecasting is crucial for managing resources, making informed decisions, and ensuring the financial health of a business.

6. **Problem-Solving:** Entrepreneurs encounter obstacles regularly. Effective problem-solving skills enable them to identify issues, analyse available options, and implement solutions.
7. **Resilience:** Resilience allows entrepreneurs to bounce back from setbacks and failures, maintaining motivation and determination throughout their journey.
8. **Negotiation:** Negotiation skills are invaluable when dealing with investors, partners, suppliers, and customers. Entrepreneurs must negotiate favourable terms and agreements.
9. **Sales and Marketing:** Effectively selling products or services and marketing them to the target audience are core entrepreneurial skills. Understanding customer needs and preferences is essential.
10. **Networking:** Building a network of mentors, advisors, peers, and industry contacts is key for gaining support, insights, and opportunities.

While all these skills are valuable, the importance of specific skills may vary depending on your business's nature and your role as an entrepreneur. It's essential to assess which skills are most relevant to your own business and focus on developing them.

At this juncture, I do think you have enough information to move on to the exercise and we will soon do so. Before we do, though, I want to make it clear that you do not need a business degree or any formal education to pursue entrepreneurship. Too often, I have seen people with good business ideas and the right skillset forego their entrepreneurial dreams thinking that they cannot succeed without formal education. There are many ways to learn and develop the skills that you need, so don't let that be a deterrent.

As much as you can succeed with formal education, which includes degrees, courses, and programs in entrepreneurship, business, or related fields, you can also succeed without. Practical experience is one option and involves hands-on involvement in entrepreneurial activities. It encompasses real-world learning through internships, startups, volunteering, or self-initiated projects. Find what works for you and the business that you want to create.

Planting the Seed

"I knew I was bigger than the box they wanted to put me in."

– Cicely Tyson

Some people say I am too 'strict' when it comes to coaching business owners; however, I rather consider myself realistic. If you have already read my entry in the book, you will note that I advise against taking on every single opportunity that comes your way. This 'strictness' stands on that premise. Not everyone who needs coaching is the right fit for me and vice versa. Without knowing what you want from your entrepreneurial journey, your why, or what your true passion is, you stand the risk of seeing no return on your investment or simply giving up when times get tough.

I am not in the business of helping people fail. Hence, I always use my self-assessment questionnaire to determine whether I will be onboarding a client or not. It helps me assess where they are and whether or not I can be of help. Technically, you have onboarded yourself on this coaching journey and have no other choice but to be successful. You have bought this workbook, are on your own, and I want you to get the most out of it. Want the same for yourself. Do the work and watch it pay off overtime.

This self-assessment will help you identify your strengths and areas where you can focus on improvement, ultimately guiding you towards a successful entrepreneurial path.

Start by completing the questionnaire and looking at your results to see what it says about your current state. The most important part of this process is that you are completely honest with yourself. No one is watching. You do not have to share your answers with anyone, so be as transparent as you can be. You will look back and be grateful that you were in a year or so when you look at your progress.

Self-Assessment Questionnaire

"You may encounter many defeats, but you must not be defeated."

– Maya Angelou

Instructions: *For each question, assign a score from 1 to 5, with 1 being "Novice" and 5 being "Expert." You can only select one score per question. Circle your answers <u>with a pencil</u>. If you do not know what something is, score it as "Novice."*

1. **How well do you understand your personal motivation and drive for entrepreneurship?**
    - 1 (Novice)
    - 2
    - 3
    - 4
    - 5 (Expert)

2. **How confident are you in articulating your business idea and its unique value proposition?**
    - 1 (Novice)
    - 2
    - 3
    - 4
    - 5 (Expert)

3. **How skilled are you in creating a vision board and mind map to define your business identity?**
    - 1 (Novice)
    - 2
    - 3
    - 4
    - 5 (Expert)

4. **How effectively can you assess your strengths and weaknesses for entrepreneurial success?**
    - 1 (Novice)
    - 2

- 3
- 4
- 5 (Expert)

5. **How proficient are you at setting SMART (Specific, Measurable, Achievable, Relevant, Time-bound) goals and action plans?**
   - 1 (Novice)
   - 2
   - 3
   - 4
   - 5 (Expert)

6. **How well can you evaluate the financial health and growth potential of your business?**
   - 1 (Novice)
   - 2
   - 3
   - 4
   - 5 (Expert)

7. **How skilled are you in conducting market research and developing customer personas?**
   - 1 (Novice)
   - 2
   - 3
   - 4
   - 5 (Expert)

8. **How confident are you in crafting a marketing and branding strategy for your business?**
   - 1 (Novice)
   - 2
   - 3
   - 4
   - 5 (Expert)

9. **How proficient are you at networking and building valuable relationships in your industry?**
   - 1 (Novice)
   - 2
   - 3
   - 4
   - 5 (Expert)

10. **How well can you manage your time and increase daily productivity?**
    - 1 (Novice)
    - 2
    - 3
    - 4
    - 5 (Expert)

11. **How experienced are you in seeking mentorship and establishing a support network for your entrepreneurial journey?**
    - 1 (Novice)
    - 2
    - 3
    - 4
    - 5 (Expert)

12. **How knowledgeable are you about the legal requirements and regulations related to your business?**
    - 1 (Novice)
    - 2
    - 3
    - 4
    - 5 (Expert)

13. **How skilled are you at creating and managing a budget for your business?**
    - 1 (Novice)
    - 2
    - 3
    - 4
    - 5 (Expert)

14. **How effective are you at adapting to changes and pivoting your business strategy when needed?**
    - 1 (Novice)
    - 2
    - 3
    - 4
    - 5 (Expert)

15. **How well can you assess market trends and identify emerging opportunities in your industry?**
    - 1 (Novice)
    - 2
    - 3

- 4
- 5 (Expert)

16. **How skilled are you at creating and delivering persuasive pitches and presentations?**
    - 1 (Novice)
    - 2
    - 3
    - 4
    - 5 (Expert)

17. **How proficient are you at managing and optimizing your business finances, including cash flow and investments?**
    - 1 (Novice)
    - 2
    - 3
    - 4
    - 5 (Expert)

18. **How knowledgeable are you about intellectual property rights and protecting your business ideas?**
    - 1 (Novice)
    - 2
    - 3
    - 4
    - 5 (Expert)

19. **How experienced are you in building a strong online presence and leveraging digital marketing?**
    - 1 (Novice)
    - 2
    - 3
    - 4
    - 5 (Expert)

20. **How confident are you in handling negotiations and securing beneficial partnerships for your business?**
    - 1 (Novice)
    - 2
    - 3
    - 4
    - 5 (Expert)

21. **How well can you identify and address potential risks and challenges in your business plan?**

- 1 (Novice)
- 2
- 3
- 4
- 5 (Expert)

22. **How skilled are you at crafting compelling business proposals and securing funding or investment?**
- 1 (Novice)
- 2
- 3
- 4
- 5 (Expert)

23. **How proficient are you at setting up and managing efficient business operations and logistics?**
- 1 (Novice)
- 2
- 3
- 4
- 5 (Expert)

24. **How experienced are you in managing a team or outsourcing tasks effectively?**
- 1 (Novice)
- 2
- 3
- 4
- 5 (Expert)

25. **How knowledgeable are you about customer service strategies and maintaining strong client relationships?**
- 1 (Novice)
- 2
- 3
- 4
- 5 (Expert)

26. **How skilled are you at staying informed about industry trends and innovations?**
- 1 (Novice)
- 2
- 3
- 4

- 5 (Expert)

27. **How proficient are you at evaluating the scalability and growth potential of your business model?**
   - 1 (Novice)
   - 2
   - 3
   - 4
   - 5 (Expert)

28. **How effective are you at managing stress and maintaining a healthy work-life balance?**
   - 1 (Novice)
   - 2
   - 3
   - 4
   - 5 (Expert)

29. **How confident are you in your ability to measure and analyse business performance using key metrics?**
   - 1 (Novice)
   - 2
   - 3
   - 4
   - 5 (Expert)

30. **How proficient are you at adapting to emerging technologies and leveraging them for your business?**
   - 1 (Novice)
   - 2
   - 3
   - 4
   - 5 (Expert)

31. **How knowledgeable are you about ethical and sustainable business practices?**
   - 1 (Novice)
   - 2
   - 3
   - 4
   - 5 (Expert)

32. **How skilled are you at fostering a positive company culture and nurturing a motivated team?**
   - 1 (Novice)

- 2
- 3
- 4
- 5 (Expert)

You've done it! Well done on scoring yourself. The next step is to calculate your score and see where you fall. Now, understand this: no matter how low your score is, I do not want you to dwell on it. All this does is prove that you need to improve in one or more areas to move ahead in your journey as a business owner. At the end of the book, after all your learning, you will have the opportunity to reassess yourself. Trust me, the greatest reward will be seeing the progress that you have made.

Now, go ahead and take a big, deep breath. Centre yourself and start adding up all your scores.

Look below to see where you fall. Then see what your score means. Tick off both your score and its interpretation. I also recommend that you write the date here (_____).

Scoring Guidelines:

- Novice: 32 - 64
- Beginner: 65 - 96
- Intermediate: 97 - 128
- Advanced: 129 - 160
- Expert: 161 - 192

Interpreting Your Score:

- *Novice*: You have a lot to learn and explore in your entrepreneurial journey.
- *Beginner*: You have some knowledge but need to build your skills.
- *Intermediate*: You are making progress and have a good foundation.
- *Advanced*: You have a strong grasp of entrepreneurship but can continue to grow.
- *Expert*: You are highly skilled and experienced in entrepreneurship.

Before you move on to the next section, let's do some reflection and affirmation.

Reflection

1. Take a moment to reflect on what initially inspired you to pursue entrepreneurship. Write down one word that sums this up:

   _____

2. Consider the challenges you anticipate and how they align with your long-term goals. Write down the three most important ones in order of importance below:

   _____

   _____

   _____

3. Now, reflect on your personal values and how they will shape your business journey. Which three do you think are most relevant in this regard. Write them down below:

   _____

   _____

   _____

Affirmation Statements

For the next few days, repeat the following affirmations to yourself. You are welcome to tweak them if you feel the need to. Stick with the theme as that's what's important.

1. I am planting the seed of my entrepreneurial journey with intention and purpose.

2. I embrace the challenges ahead as opportunities for growth.

3. My values guide me, ensuring that my business aligns with my authentic self.

Nurturing Growth

"Success is no accident. It is hard work, perseverance, learning, studying, sacrifice, and most of all, love of what you are doing."

– Peju Alatise

The exercises that you will be completing in the next two sections are what I usually refer to as the heart of one's entrepreneurial journey. This is where growth takes root and eventually flourishes. Just as the farmer tills and nourishes the soil to yield a bountiful harvest, this section of the workbook invites you to cultivate your potential as an entrepreneur.

Completing the questionnaire in the previous section was merely planting the seed. The exercise helped you assess what your 'soil' looks like now – it was a self-discovery exercise. Now, you need that seed to grow. By the end of this workbook, you must be able to go back to that seed and assess its growth.

Much like the farmer's young sapling reaching for the sun, you'll explore how to shape and define your business identity. This identity, encompassing your brand's essence, values, target audience, and unique selling propositions, will serve as the heart and soul of your business.

Now, as you embark on this leg of your journey, remember that nurturing growth is an art. It requires patience, care, and a deep understanding of the unique qualities that make you different from all the other entrepreneurs out there. With each exercise, you'll find yourself growing closer to the heights you've envisioned for your business. So, embrace this phase of growth with open arms, knowing that it's the nurturing of your entrepreneurial potential that will ultimately lead to the success that you aspire achieving.

Let's start off with the first exercise in this section on the next page.

Self-Reflection Exercise: Discovering Your Entrepreneurial Drive and Values

"The only way to do great work is to love what you do."

– Condoleezza Rice

I consider self-awareness to be one of the most powerful tools for success. This exercise is designed to help you gain clarity about your aspirations, motivations, and the values that you hold dear as an entrepreneur. Find a quiet space, and let's begin.

Step 1: The Origin Story

This exercise should take you about 15 to 20 minutes to complete. Try not to overthink. There is no such thing as the perfect answer to any of the questions that I pose in this workbook.

Think back to the moment when you first considered becoming an entrepreneur. What sparked this idea? Was there a specific incident, person, or experience that planted the seed of entrepreneurship in your mind? Write down the story of how it all began.

_____
_____
_____
_____
_____
_____
_____
_____
_____
_____
_____
_____
_____

Step 2: The Why

I recommend spending another 10 to 20 minutes on this activity. If you get stuck, come back to it later.

Reflect on the reasons driving you to pursue your business dreams. Please, do not minimize your pursuit to making money. We ALL, as business people, want to make money but for those of us who are successful, we have a why that far outweighs the money.

If making money is the only reason that you want to run your own business, it is not enough. You will fail before you even start. No business makes an unlimited supply of money 365 days per year, and neither will yours. When you have a good enough reason why you are in business, you will refuse to give up when your profits are low and your expenditures higher. This is the why that you need to focus on.

Ask yourself the following questions and write down your answers:

Why do I want to be an entrepreneur?

_____
_____
_____
_____
_____
_____
_____

What do I hope to achieve personally and professionally?

_____
_____
_____
_____
_____
_____
_____

What impact do I want to make in the world through my business?

_____
_____
_____
_____
_____
_____
_____
_____
_____

Now, write down your single most profound motivation for becoming an entrepreneur in one short sentence or three words:

_____
_____

That is your why. **Mark this page.** Every time you think of giving up on your business, I want you to come back to this page and remind yourself of why you want to run your own business. If you want to take it a step further, get creative and make some form of wall art with your why on it. Hang it where you can see it often and especially when you need a reminder. I have mine just across from my desk in my home office and in an A4 frame on my desk at work.

Step 3: Values Exploration

This is possibly where you will spend the bulk of your time in this section. I recommend about 30 minutes.

Consider the core values that guide your life and business decisions. I want you to really think about this if you don't already know what your core values are.

Values help us navigate our entrepreneurial journey more than we realise. The decisions we make and how we do things are often rooted in the same values. Create a list of your top five values. Let me use myself as an example to help you get started. I value integrity; I should not have to be in the office for my staff to get their work done. I value creativity; nothing irks me more than having to think for my entire team. I value freedom above almost everything else; being able to do what I want when I want is important to me. I value customer satisfaction; "… Be the labour great or small, do it well or not at all." I value finding joy in my work; whatever the job is, I must be able to enjoy it… You should get the idea by now.

It's your turn. Write down your five values and describe why each value is important to you and how it aligns with your entrepreneurial goals.

_____
_____
_____
_____
_____
_____
_____
_____
_____
_____
_____
_____
_____
_____
_____

Step 4: Overcoming Challenges

If you've managed to read through the **Great Entrepreneurs** book already, you've seen how entrepreneurs continue to overcome challenges both in their personal and business lives. All it takes is your willingness. Once you are willing to find solutions to the problems you face, everything else pretty much falls into place — because you do the work necessary.

Recall the challenges and obstacles you've encountered on your entrepreneurial path thus far. If you haven't set up your business yet, think about what's getting in your way. Otherwise, look at your personal life. How did you face those challenges, and what did you learn from them? Share specific instances and the lessons you've learned.

_____
_____
_____
_____
_____
_____
_____
_____
_____
_____
_____
_____
_____
_____
_____
_____
_____
_____
_____
_____
_____
_____
_____
_____

Reflecting on these challenges, how have they shaped your journey?

In essence, how have the lessons learned affected the way you think about business or your business?

_____
_____
_____
_____
_____
_____
_____
_____
_____
_____
_____
_____
_____
_____
_____
_____
_____
_____
_____
_____
_____
_____
_____
_____
_____
_____
_____
_____
_____
_____
_____
_____

Step 5: Your Vision Statement

If all you have for your business thus far is an idea, I want you to spend more time on this exercise. Think about things carefully, but do not try to make your vision statement perfect. You can always come back to it later, once you have done all your research and decided on the exact activities that your business will perform. Spend up to 15 minutes on this exercise for now.

Craft a vision statement for your business or entrepreneurial journey (it might be that you want to own multiple businesses). Envision the future you aspire to create through your business. Describe not only what you want to achieve but also how you want to feel and the impact you want to have. Use vivid language and imagery.

_____
_____
_____
_____
_____
_____
_____
_____
_____
_____
_____
_____
_____
_____
_____
_____
_____
_____
_____
_____
_____
_____
_____

Step 6: Action Commitment

Now, let's bring everything together. Review everything that you've written in this section thus far. Take note of the insights and realizations you've had about yourself and your business journey.

What actionable steps can you take to align your actions more closely with your values and motivations? Set at least three concrete goals or actions based on your reflections.

_____
_____
_____
_____
_____
_____
_____
_____
_____
_____
_____
_____
_____
_____
_____
_____
_____
_____
_____
_____
_____
_____
_____
_____
_____
_____
_____
_____
_____
_____

Word of Advice

Self-reflection is an ongoing practice. Periodically revisit your responses to remind yourself of your motivations, values, and vision. Embrace your unique journey as an entrepreneur, and remember that your story and path are inspirations to others as it should be to yourself.

Defining Your Business Identity: Vision Board and Mind Map

"Your ability to communicate is an important tool in your pursuit of your goals, whether it is with your family, your co-workers, or your clients and customers."

– Oprah Winfrey

Your business identity encompasses your brand's essence, values, target audience, and unique selling propositions. In this exercise, we'll explore creative ways to define your business identity using a vision board and a mind map. Sometimes it is just not enough to keep our ideas and goals in our thoughts. Seeing them daily serves as constant reminders, which can fuel motivation — literally being the fuel we need to keep going.

On the next page, I have added a sample vision board, which I created in Canva. You could also choose to create your own on a similar platform on your computer. Note that the one I share in this workbook is very limited in many ways. I have just added a few of the goals I have for my own business. My actual vision board is much more extensive. Be audacious in coming up with your own.

Sample Vision Board

It's time to create your own. Let's start by getting everything you need together. Remember that you can use an online platform or even MS Word or PowerPoint then print out your creation. See what works best for you. Otherwise, get the following materials below and let's get creative!

Materials Needed:

- Poster board or a large piece of paper
- Magazines, images, and words that resonate with your brand
- Coloured markers, pens, or pencils
- Sticky notes or index cards
- Glue or tape

Step 1: Visual Inspiration

Okay, so you should have some form of idea of where you want to be in business and what you want to achieve overall. With this in mind, begin by browsing through magazines, online images, or any visual materials that resonate with your business identity. If you can draw, put that skill to work. Otherwise, look for images, colours, and words that evoke the essence of your brand. Cut them out or save them digitally. Do not delay doing this (waiting to find just the right images). Try to complete this part of the task within 30 minutes.

Step 2: Vision Board Creation

On your poster board or large paper, start arranging the visuals you've collected in a collage-like fashion. Be creative and let your intuition guide you. Include images that represent your brand's mission, values, and the emotions you want to evoke in your audience/customers. Dedicate no more than 40 minutes to this step.

Step 3: Values Exploration

Moving on to the next step in this exercise, I want you to dedicate 20 minutes and no more to this task. Do not get bogged down.

Take a moment to reflect on the core values of your business or the core values that you mentioned earlier in the workbook if you do not yet have an established business. What principles and beliefs are at the foundation of your entrepreneurial journey? Write down your values on sticky notes or index cards.

Step 4: Incorporate Values

Use the next 30 minutes to integrate your core values into your vision board. Place your value cards strategically among the visuals. Connect each value to specific images or words that illustrate how they are embodied in your brand. In the example that I showed you, you will notice that I put a picture of a handshake with the customer satisfaction sticker.

That's it! You have created your own vision board! Well done. Don't worry if it isn't *perfect*. Consider it a start. Stick with this board for at least a year. This gives you the chance to tick things off your board and make room for growth. I also suggest that you update your board or create a new one every 12 months. If you haven't achieved every goal that you've set for your business, add the ones left over to the next year's vision board along with new ones. Ensure that you have a minimum of three new goals added each year and work hard to tick off as many as possible.

If you still have gas left in the tank, you can move on to the next part of this task. Otherwise, go ahead and pause for now. Try to come back within three days. Do not allow yourself the luxury of putting off your dreams.

Mind Map Creation

Welcome back! I hope you are ready for the final two steps of this exercise. It's time to work on your mind map.

Create a mind map that outlines your brand's identity. In the centre of the paper, write your business name or a central theme that represents your brand. Branch out from the centre with keywords, phrases, and images that symbolize your target audience, unique selling points, and brand essence. Look at the example that I have created on the next page, then go ahead and give it a go. Note that I have not shown the full mind map. You can also look at similar ones online for inspiration.

I have left a full page for you to create your mind map inside this workbook. Start there. Once you are satisfied with it, transfer it to a poster board. Let your creative juice flow!

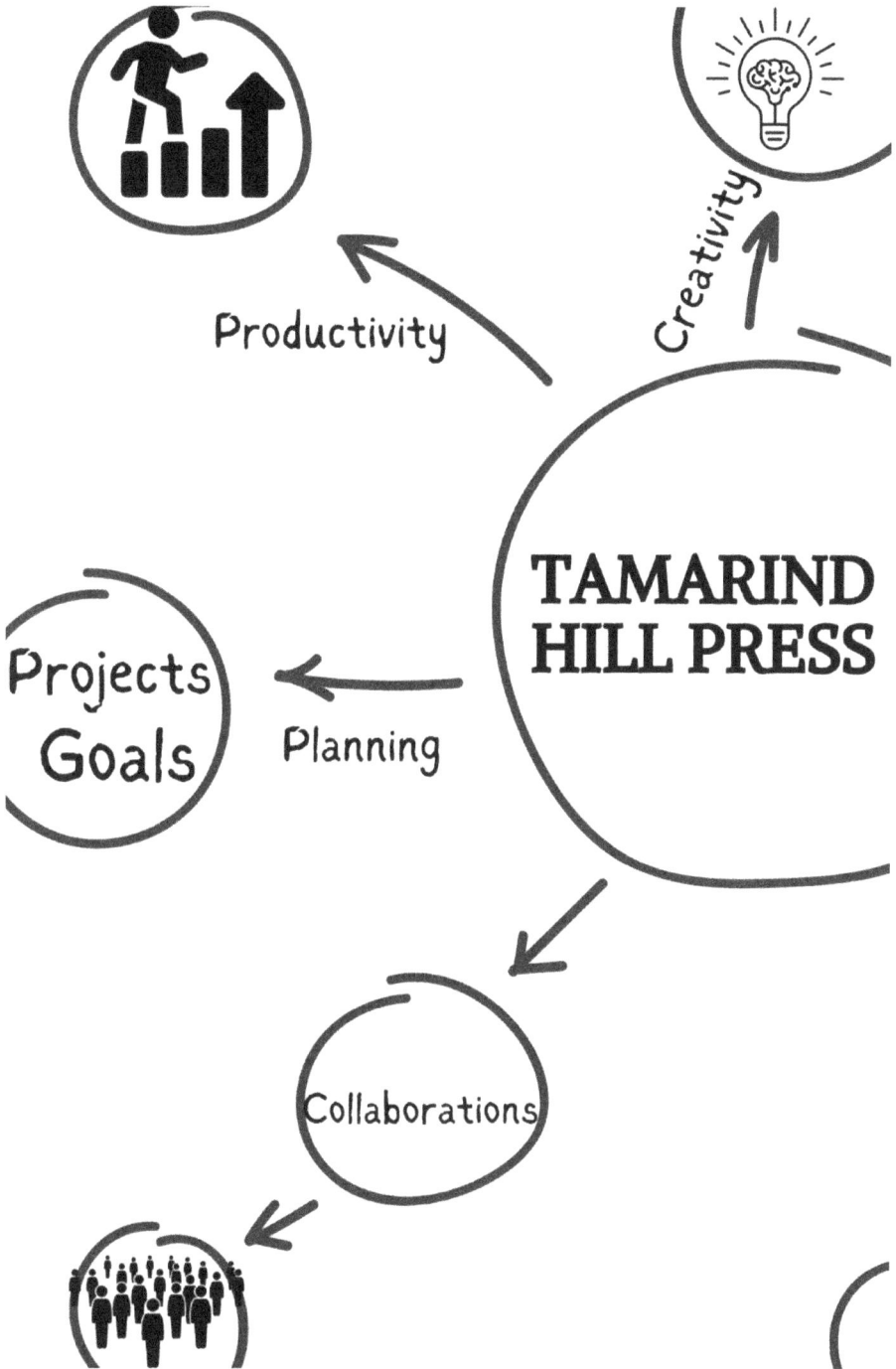

Productivity

Creativity

Projects Goals

Planning

TAMARIND HILL PRESS

Collaborations

My Mind Map

Display and Reflect

Look at you showing up for yourself and your dreams! You are doing a great job and have come a long way. It's time to take the final step.

Now that you've completed your vision board and mind map, find a prominent place to display them in your workspace or home. Ensure you can see them daily to remind yourself of your brand's identity and values.

That's it, you have completed this exercise. I am proud of you and I hope you are too.

Your vision board and mind map are powerful tools to help keep your business identity at the forefront of your mind. They serve as constant reminders of your brand's essence, values, and mission. Continue to refer back to these visual representations to stay aligned with your unique business identity.

Word of Advice

Keep your mind map and vision board visible and accessible. Do not fool yourself into thinking that you will pull them out of your desk drawer often enough. If you see them daily, they will continue to remind you of the things that you have to do and why. I have several vision boards and ensure that they are ALL visible. They help keep me on track.

You have successfully completed the Nurturing Growth section of the workbook. Before moving on, let's reflect and affirm.

Reflection

1. Reflect on the discoveries you've made about your entrepreneurial drive and values. What two things stand out the most to you? (What have you learned about yourself?)

_____
_____
_____
_____
_____
_____

_____

_____

_____

Affirmation Statements

1. I continue to nurture my entrepreneurial growth with self-compassion, self-awareness, and self-discovery.

2. My business identity is a reflection of my vision, values, and the unique offerings that I make in my field.

Branching Out

"There is no greater agony than bearing an untold story inside you."

– Maya Angelou

Sticking to the idea of the farmer planting a seed, this section of the process is where you will begin to truly blossom as an entrepreneur. In the preceding sections, you've carefully sown the seeds of your entrepreneurial aspirations and nurtured them with self-discovery. Essentially, you were 'tilling the soil;' assessing the quality beneath your feet. Now, the time has come to watch those seeds grow and flourish.

Just as a tree's branches symbolize its expansion and vitality, in this section, you'll explore how to expand your horizons and define your business identity in even more details. 'Branching Out' is both an art and a science. It's about creativity, strategy, and adaptability. Each exercise will help to push you closer to the heights you've envisioned for your business.

Remember that with every exercise, you're crafting the branches of a thriving and flourishing entrepreneurial future. So, as you move to the next page, envision your journey as a tree extending its branches toward new opportunities and possibilities. There is absolutely nothing that you cannot do.

Strengths and Weaknesses Assessment

"You have to have confidence in your ability, and then be tough enough to follow through."

– Rosalynn Carter

Self-awareness is one of the many qualities that will help you succeed in entrepreneurship. Knowing your strengths allows you to amplify them, while understanding your weaknesses helps you identify areas for growth and improvement. In this exercise, we'll delve deep into the qualities that you possess and how they will help you build a successful business. I usually ask my clients to take 90 minutes to two hours to complete this exercise. Just try to finish it in one sitting. Write down what comes to mind first as that's usually the best and most honest answer.

Step 1: Recognizing Your Strengths

What are the qualities, skills, and characteristics that set you apart and drive your success? These do not have to be business related, and you can write down as many as you wish. Think about this in general terms. Be honest and specific.

Example of Strengths:
1. Exceptional problem-solving skills
2. Strong leadership abilities
3. Effective communication
4. Innovative thinking

Write down your strengths:

_____
_____
_____
_____
_____
_____

_____

_____

_____

_____

_____

Step 2: Leveraging Your Strengths

For each strength you've listed above, consider how you can leverage it to the benefit of your business. Think about specific actions or strategies you can implement to make the most of your strengths. Write down practical steps.

Example of Leveraging Strengths:

If "effective communication" is a strength, consider using it to enhance customer relationships, develop persuasive marketing materials, and foster collaboration within your team.

_____

_____

_____

_____

_____

_____

_____

_____

_____

_____

_____

_____

_____

_____

_____

_____

_____

_____

_____

_____

Step 3: Acknowledging Your Weaknesses

Don't be turned off. We all have them, and the more honest we are about our weaknesses, the better able we are to turn them into strengths. Now, it's time to assess your weaknesses honestly.

Example of Weaknesses:
1. Difficulty with time management
2. Limited financial expertise
3. Struggle with delegation
4. Fear of public speaking
5. Inconsistent networking efforts

Thinking about the different areas of entrepreneurship that you find challenging, what skills or qualities do you need to improve? Write down your weaknesses:

_____
_____
_____
_____
_____
_____
_____
_____
_____
_____
_____
_____
_____
_____
_____
_____
_____
_____
_____
_____

Step 4: Improving Your Weaknesses

Now, for each weakness you've identified, brainstorm ways to work on improving or mitigating it. Consider resources, courses, or mentors that can help you overcome these challenges. Write down actionable steps.

Example of Improving Weaknesses:

If "difficulty with time management" is a weakness, consider using time management apps, taking a course on time management, or seeking guidance from a mentor.

_____

_____

_____

_____

_____

_____

_____

_____

_____

_____

_____

_____

_____

_____

_____

_____

_____

_____

_____

_____

_____

_____

_____

_____

_____

_____

Step 5: Creating a Growth Plan

Before we close off this exercise, I need you to do one more thing. It's time to develop a growth plan that outlines how you will capitalize on your strengths and address your weaknesses. I do not want you to focus on all of them at once as you might end up not making any progress in the timeframe and decide to abandon your growth plan all together. Choose *one strength and one weakness* to work on.

You should have already written down the steps for each. Now, go into more detail and create a timeline for those steps. **What will you do, and when?** Set deadlines and do the work that you promise to do to ensure that you achieve what you've set out to in the next six months. At the end of the six months, you should have improved on or completely gotten rid of your weakness. Additionally, you should have leveraged your strength to benefit your business. Once you have worked on those, choose another strength and a weakness to work on for the next three to six months. Keep doing this until you have leveraged all your strengths and improved all your weaknesses.

Use the table on the next few pages to develop your growth plan.

My Growth Plan

STRENGTH		WEAKNESS	
Step	When	Step	When

Word of Advice

Having strengths and weaknesses remain a part of who we are; I suppose this will be the case until our last breath. As we learn, we grow and develop strengths. Likewise, there is so much that we do not yet know and improvements that we will always need to make; our weak areas. Thus, as an entrepreneur, your ability to evolve and adapt is a key factor in your success.

The exercise you have completed is a starting point for personal and professional growth. I suggest that you revisit it periodically to track your progress. See what strengths you have leveraged for the benefit of your business and which weaknesses you have improved or gotten rid of.

I believe in continuous improvement. The moment we stop learning, life, in my opinion, becomes dull. So, every year, I take time out in the last few days of December to assess my strengths and weaknesses. This is when I plan which courses I will be taking and how I will develop for the following year. Think about doing something similar to help you, not just in business but in life.

Goal Setting and Action Planning: Turning Dreams into Reality

"I don't believe in giving up. I'm a person who just keeps fighting and keeps going."

– Gabby Douglas

Goals provide us with direction and purpose. If we know why we are doing something, what our goal is, it keeps us on track. Thus, goal setting and action planning are important aspects of developing your entrepreneurial skills.

In this exercise, we'll set clear and inspiring short-term and long-term goals for your business. Then, we'll break down each goal into actionable steps, complete with deadlines. Finally, we'll create a visual timeline to keep you on track.

Step 1: Define Your Goals

Set aside about 20 minutes to complete this exercise. Begin by thinking about your business's future. What do you want to achieve in the short term (3-6 months) and the long term (1-3 years)? Be specific, and consider both financial and non-financial objectives.

Example of Short-term Goals (3-6 months):
1. Increase monthly revenue by 20%.
2. Launch my business or a new product line.
3. Expand my company's customer base by 15%.

Example of Long-term Goals (1-3 years):
1. Achieve profitability and sustainable growth.
2. Establish a presence in three new markets.
3. Develop a strong online community of loyal customers.

Write down three goals for each timeframe:

_____
_____
_____
_____
_____
_____
_____
_____
_____
_____
_____
_____
_____
_____
_____
_____
_____
_____
_____
_____
_____
_____
_____
_____
_____
_____
_____
_____
_____
_____
_____
_____
_____

Step 2: Break Down Your Goals

Spend another 20 minutes on this part of the exercise. Take one short-term and one long-term goal from the list you've just created. Break each goal down into actionable steps. Consider what needs to happen to achieve these goals. Include specific actions, resources needed, and potential challenges.

Example of this Breakdown: Short-term Goal - Increase monthly revenue by 20%:
Launch a new marketing campaign, targeting existing and potential customers.
- **Action**: Create compelling marketing materials and ads.
- **Deadline**: Within 2 weeks.
- **Resources**: Marketing materials, advertising budget, marketing team or freelancers, data and analytics tools, project management tools, marketing calendar, ad spend tracking system, etc.
- **Potential Challenges**: Content quality issues, technical issues like website glitches, insufficient funds for a robust marketing campaign, etc.

Short-term Goal:			
Actions to Take	**Deadline**	**Resources Needed**	**Potential Challenges**

Long-term Goal:			
Actions to Take	Deadline	Resources Needed	Potential Challenges

Step 3: Visual Timeline

To make things more exciting, it's time to create a visual timeline to map out your goals and action steps. You can use a large poster or a digital tool for this. Draw a timeline that spans your short-term and long-term goals. Add milestones for each actionable step with corresponding deadlines.

Example of a Visual Timeline

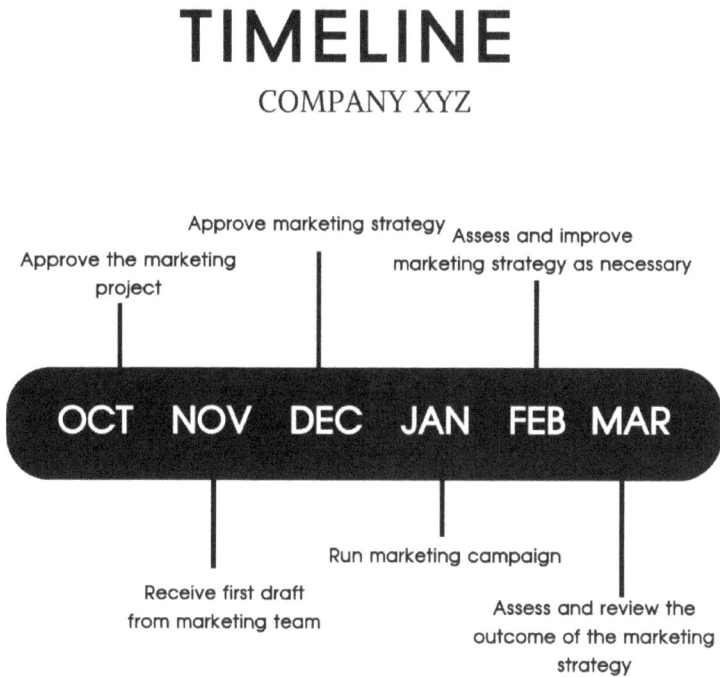

TIMELINE
COMPANY XYZ

Approve marketing strategy
Assess and improve marketing strategy as necessary

Approve the marketing project

OCT NOV DEC JAN FEB MAR

Run marketing campaign

Receive first draft from marketing team

Assess and review the outcome of the marketing strategy

GOAL Increase monthly revenue by 20%

BUDGET £4000.00

My Visual Timeline

Create your own here.

Word of Advice

Periodically revisit your goals, action steps, and visual timeline. Assess your progress, celebrate your achievements (I purchase something my business needs to celebrate each achievement), and adjust your plans as needed. Stay adaptable and committed to your goals.

You have branched out! Well done, you. Let's reflect and affirm.

Reflection

1. Without going back to what you wrote down, write down three things you remember from the strengths and weaknesses you've identified within yourself.

   _____

   _____

   _____

Affirmation Statements

1. I embrace my strengths and acknowledge my weaknesses as opportunities for improvement.

2. My goals are set, my path is clear, and success is within my reach.

3. My visual timeline reminds me that I am making steady progress toward my dreams.

Bearing Fruit

"Financial education is the great equalizer. It empowers you to take control of your destiny and make choices that align with your values and aspirations."

– Mellody Hobson

Finally, the seeds you've sown, nurtured, and diligently tended to are finally ready to bear fruit. Your efforts in the previous sections have primed you for this.

Bearing fruit is not just about immediate gains but also about sustainable growth and long-term success. These fruits are the tangible expressions of all the work that you've put in. Its reward for your investment in yourself.

Let's jump into the next set of exercises so you can begin to taste the sweet rewards of your labour.

Financial Health Check

"It's not the absence of fear, it's overcoming it. Sometimes you've got to blast through and have faith."

– Emma Emeozor

Understanding the finance and the financial health of your business is crucial for making informed decisions and steering your business towards success. If you are yet to start your business, I suggest saving the bulk of this exercise for the first six months post launch. Otherwise, go ahead and complete this exercise.

In this exercise, we'll review the essential financial statements — balance sheet, income statement, and cash flow statement. We'll analyse revenue, expenses, and cash flow, and identify areas for improvement. Finally, we'll set financial goals for the next quarter.

Step 1: Review Financial Statements

It is not enough for your accountant to know what is going on in your business financially. It is also your responsibility. Do not make "I don't like numbers" an excuse. If any problem arises with your finances, the government will come after you as the business owner, so it is worth understanding what is going on with your business's finances.

If you do not already have some accounting background, look at taking a course or reading a book or two to develop your knowledge. Here's a trick: get the secondary/high school accounting textbook in your country and start reading. It is a very good starting point and where I built the foundation for my accounting knowledge years ago after reading the book cover to cover, doing the exercises in two months, and sitting the GCSE exam a few months later. It was just a book to read because I had access to it, but then I wanted to test whether I understood what I'd learned. I passed the exam after not picking up the book for months. If you like money, the knowledge will stick. Give it a try. You do not have to go take the exam or even work all the problems in the book, but at least try to understand the different accounting terms and what they mean.

I have also added some terms at the back of this workbook to help you start building your accounting knowledge.

Accounting knowledge in your back pocket, it is now time to gather and review your balance sheet, income statement, and cash flow statement for the previous quarter or year. Familiarize yourself with the terminology and key metrics in each statement.

Write down those key terms and metrics below. If there is something that you do not understand, write it down. Look into it and make notes here as well.

_____
_____
_____
_____
_____
_____
_____
_____
_____
_____
_____
_____
_____
_____
_____
_____
_____
_____
_____
_____
_____
_____
_____
_____

Step 2: Analyse Revenue, Expenses, and Cash Flow

Examine your revenue sources and patterns (where your money comes from and when). Identify your main revenue streams and assess their growth or decline. Analyse your major expense categories and track any significant changes. Evaluate your cash flow trends, identifying periods of surplus or deficit.

Example Analysis:
- **Revenue**: Identify which products or services generate the most revenue and if there are seasonal trends (e.g., I sell more books in March and December of each year).
- **Expenses**: Categorize expenses (e.g., fixed, variable) and identify areas where you can reduce costs. Fixed expenses could be the leasing fee on your business car, while variable expenses could be the fuel whose price changes depending on different market factors.
- **Cash Flow**: Analyse when cash inflows and outflows occur. You might collect most of your income from customers at the end of the month and also pay out more money for all your business expenses at the end of the month. Identify any irregularities or patterns. An irregularity could be realising that your accountant has left off a zero off a number or added one too many. Both scenarios can be detrimental, hence your NEED to like numbers. Patters could be the same example of when you pay out the most and receive the most income in each month.

Go ahead and use the space over the next two pages to write down as much as you understand from your accounting documents.

_____
_____
_____
_____
_____
_____
_____
_____
_____
_____

Step 3: Identify Areas for Improvement

Based on your analysis, pinpoint areas in your revenue generation, expense management, and/or cash flow where improvements can be made. Consider both short-term and long-term improvements.

Example of Areas for Improvement:
- **Revenue**: Explore new markets or diversify products to increase revenue streams.
- **Expenses**: Negotiate better rates with suppliers to reduce the cost of goods sold.
- **Cash Flow**: Implement better invoicing and payment tracking systems to improve cash flow.

_____
_____
_____
_____
_____
_____
_____
_____
_____
_____
_____
_____
_____
_____
_____
_____
_____
_____
_____
_____
_____
_____

Step 4: Set Financial Goals for the Next Quarter

Based on your analysis and identified areas for improvement, I want you to now take some time to set achievable financial goals for the next quarter. Ensure your goals are:

- **Specific** (What exactly do you want to achieve?)
- **Measurable** (How will you measure it; in this case, it could be in terms of the amount of money you want to make.)
- **Achievable** (If your highest month's income is £500, do not set a goal of making £10,000 in the next month; be more realistic.)
- **Relevant** (It must be in line with the desired growth of your business based on your assessment.)
- **Time-bound** (Write down the date that you want to achieve each goal by.)

This is SMART goal setting.

Example of SMART Financial Goals:
Increase revenue by 15% through a targeted marketing campaign by December 31, 2023.

_____
_____
_____
_____
_____
_____
_____
_____
_____
_____
_____
_____
_____
_____
_____
_____

Word of Advice

Continually assess, improve, and prosper financially. Get to know as much as you can about the financial aspects of your business.

Market Research and Customer Persona Development: Navigating Your Target Audience

"I feel like in life, we're all just trying to be the best version of ourselves."

– Zendaya

A target market refers to a specific group of consumers or businesses that a company aims to reach with its products and/or services. This group is characterized by shared characteristics, needs, preferences, and behaviours that make them more likely to be interested in and responsive to the company's offerings. Therefore, identifying and understanding its target market is a fundamental aspect of a company's marketing strategy.

In this exercise, we'll delve into market research and customer persona development. This is where you get the opportunity to gain insights into your industry and create detailed customer personas to guide your marketing efforts.

Step 1: Industry Market Research

Start by researching your industry to understand its current trends, challenges, and opportunities. Analyse competitors, market size, and growth potential. Gather information from reputable sources such as industry reports, trade publications, and online databases.

Keep a folder with the information that you have collected. These details are essential for your business proposal; one of the main documents that investors and lenders require to give you money to help your business grow.

Step 2: Target Market Identification

You've done your research, now it's time to define your target market by considering who your ideal customers are. Think about demographics (age, gender, location), psychographics (interests, values, lifestyle), and any specific pain points they might have. Write down your initial thoughts:

_____
_____
_____
_____
_____
_____
_____
_____
_____
_____
_____
_____
_____
_____
_____
_____
_____
_____
_____
_____
_____
_____
_____
_____
_____
_____
_____
_____
_____
_____
_____
_____

Step 3: Conduct Customer Surveys and Interviews

Create a survey or conduct interviews with current and potential customers to gather valuable insights. If you do not have friends and family, or people around, who you think can help you with this process, get out there and try to find as many people as possible. There are people who will be willing to help. Ask questions about their needs, preferences, and challenges related to your product or service. Take note of their responses.

Step 4: Customer Persona Creation

Based on the information gathered in your survey, create detailed customer personas representing your ideal customers. Include demographics, behaviours, pain points, preferences, and even a fictional name and image to humanize the persona. Be as specific as possible.

Example of a Customer Persona:
- Name: Tina
- Age: 32
- Location: Newton Aycliffe
- Occupation: Marketing Manager
- Pain Points: Limited time to invest in writing her book, struggles with work-life balance, values high quality written work, prefers to get everything done in one place so she doesn't have to spend time searching for multiple services, and appreciates deadlines being met.

_____
_____
_____
_____
_____
_____
_____
_____
_____
_____
_____

Step 5: Tailor Marketing Efforts

Now that you have your customer personas, brainstorm strategies for tailoring your marketing efforts to resonate with each persona. Consider messaging, channels, and content that will appeal to their specific needs and preferences.

Example of Tailoring Marketing Efforts:

For 'Tina,' focus on convenience, highlight additional services that she requires, and emphasize our company's track record in meeting deadlines in our marketing materials. With Tina being so busy, we want to reach her through email marketing. Once she expresses interest, instead of setting up a physical meeting, we will create a 90 seconds pitch video for her to review on her own time.

_____
_____
_____
_____
_____
_____
_____
_____
_____
_____
_____
_____
_____
_____
_____
_____
_____
_____
_____
_____
_____

Step 6: Test and Refine

The final step is to implement your tailored marketing strategies and closely monitor their effectiveness. Use analytics tools to track customer engagement and conversions. Be prepared to refine your strategies based on real-world results. Use this space to write down notes on how you will tailor your marketing strategies moving forward:

_____

_____

_____

_____

_____

_____

_____

_____

_____

_____

_____

_____

_____

_____

_____

_____

_____

_____

_____

_____

_____

_____

_____

_____

_____

_____

_____

_____

Word of Advice

To ensure your business stays aligned with your target audience's needs and preferences, continue to conduct market research and customer persona development. There are many ways to do this, one being looking at who buys your products or uses your services. Assess this free information and develop and tailor your marketing efforts accordingly.

Marketing and Branding Strategy

"You are your best thing."

– Toni Morrison

A well-defined marketing and branding strategy is the compass that drives a business towards its goals. If you get that right, you have won half the battle. Good marketing and branding will have clients coming your way over and again.

In this exercise, you'll create a one-page marketing and branding strategy that encapsulates your unique value proposition, target audience, marketing channels, messaging, and key success metrics. I know; it is a mouthful. Don't worry, though. I'll guide you through it in a few digestible steps. Let's go!

Step 1: Unique Value Proposition

The 'numbers stuff' is out of the way, so I'll get right back to timing you for tasks in this section. For this first task, I want you to dedicate only 20 minutes to it. Remember, we do not have the time to overthink and delay our progress, so we can only dedicate so much time to it.

Start by defining your unique value proposition (UVP). What sets your business apart from competitors?

_____
_____
_____
_____
_____
_____
_____
_____
_____
_____
_____

What problem does your product or service solve, and what benefits does it offer?

_____

_____

_____

_____

_____

_____

_____

_____

_____

_____

Now, write a concise statement that captures your UVP.

Example of a UVP:

Celebrate your story, perfect your prose: our expert editing elevates your authorial voice.

_____

_____

_____

_____

_____

_____

_____

_____

_____

_____

_____

_____

_____

_____

Step 2: Target Audience

Now, take another 20 minutes to identify your ideal customers by considering demographics, psychographics, and behavioural traits. Who are they, and what motivates them? Create a detailed profile of your target audience. (**Note**: You should have already done your market research in a previous exercise.)

Example of a Target Audience Profile:
- **Demographics**: Women aged 25-40, urban dwellers, middle to high income.
- **Psychographics**: Health-conscious, environmentally aware, value convenience.
- **Behavioural Traits**: Frequent online shoppers, active on social media.

_____
_____
_____
_____
_____
_____
_____
_____
_____
_____
_____
_____
_____
_____
_____
_____
_____
_____
_____
_____
_____
_____

Step 3: Marketing Channels

Determine which marketing channels are most effective for reaching your target audience. Consider online (e.g., social media, email marketing, website), offline (e.g., events, print media), and any emerging channels relevant to your industry.

Example of Marketing Channels:
- **Social Media**: Instagram, LinkedIn, TikTok
- **Email Marketing**: Weekly newsletters with product updates and tips
- **Influencer Collaborations**: Partner with health and sustainability influencers

_____
_____
_____
_____
_____
_____
_____
_____
_____
_____
_____
_____
_____
_____
_____
_____
_____
_____
_____
_____
_____
_____
_____
_____
_____

Step 4: Messaging and Brand Voice

This can be tricky, but once you 'spot the difference,' you know exactly what it means and will find it easy to create your own. Think about big brands like 'Maxhosa Africa,' whose brand voice is rooted in celebrating the cultural richness of the South African Black community. Just like them, your brand voice should authentically reflect your values and resonate with your target audience, creating a strong and lasting connection. Let's look at another example of messaging...

Example Messaging:
- **Tagline**: "Empowering Health and Sustainability, One Product at a Time."
- **Brand Voice**: Friendly, informative, and eco-conscious.

With that in mind, craft a clear and consistent messaging strategy. Define the tone and style of your brand voice. What key messages resonate with your target audience? Develop a tagline or key messaging points. (Spend about 15 minutes on this. *You can update it later.*)

_____
_____
_____
_____
_____
_____
_____
_____
_____
_____
_____
_____
_____
_____
_____
_____
_____
_____
_____
_____

Step 5: Measuring Success

With any marketing strategy, the goal is to achieve one thing or another. Whether your campaign is aimed at increasing sales or building brand awareness, it is important that you put some form of measure in place. These can be referred to as the key performance indicators (KPIs). In essence, decide on how you will determine the success of your campaign. Will you measure it by website traffic, sales, conversion rates, etc.?

Example of KPIs and Goals:
- Increase website traffic by 20% within six months.
- Achieve a 5% monthly growth in social media followers.
- Maintain a 10% conversion rate for email subscribers.

Outline how you'll measure the success of your marketing efforts:

_____
_____
_____
_____
_____
_____
_____
_____
_____
_____
_____
_____
_____
_____
_____
_____
_____
_____
_____
_____

Step 6: One-Page Strategy

You have done a great job thus far; just one more step before you complete this exercise. I recommend that you dedicate 45 to 60 minutes to completing this task.

Compile all the elements of your marketing and branding strategy into a visually engaging one-page document. Use graphics, charts, and concise text to convey the strategy clearly and attractively. (Tip: Similar to your vision board!)

Get through that and you are finished with this task. You are one step closer to becoming a *Great Entrepreneur*! Use the page provided or create it on a paper that you'd prefer to hang in your workspace.

Word of Advice: Your one-page marketing and branding strategy is a living document that should guide your marketing efforts and ensure alignment with your business goals. Periodically review and update it as your business evolves. Yes, I have said it so many times before, but I'll say it again: Keep it where you can see it.

Networking and Relationship Building: Expanding Your Circle of Influence

"Your network is your net worth. The relationships you build can open doors, create opportunities, and help you achieve your business goals."

– Shellye Archambeau

Building a strong professional network is essential for business growth. In completing this exercise, you'll actively engage in networking by planning to attend two events within the next month. You'll also craft a compelling elevator pitch to introduce yourself and your business, and practice the crucial follow-up process.

Step 1: Event Selection

Dedicate an hour at maximum to this task. Any more and you will end up not finding or choosing an event to attend; this task is quite important, so let's not procrastinate.

Begin by researching upcoming networking events in your industry or local community. Identify two of those events that align with your business goals and target audience. For example, if you are a salon owner, see if there are any events specifically for salon owners or find an event where you can meet clients like a wedding show, or even one where businesses in your area will be coming together.

Register for these events and mark them on your calendar. If you have to pay a fee, look at all the benefits and see if they align with your short term goals. If they do and you can afford the event, then go. Ensure there is no overlap and don't double book. You must stay committed and attend these two events.

Write down the two events, the dates, and what you hope to gain from attending in the table provided on the next page.

Event Name	Event Date	Why Attend

Step 2: Elevator Pitch Development

Spend another 30 minutes on this task. Craft a concise and compelling elevator pitch. Your pitch should introduce you, your business, and the value you offer in a clear and engaging manner. Practice until you can deliver it confidently in 30-60 seconds.

Example of an Elevator Pitch:

Hi, I'm Kemone, and I'm the founder and CEO of Tamarind Hill Press — a dynamic UK-based company specializing in book publishing, top-notch editing services (with a 95% client satisfaction rate), and corporate training to enhance English communication. We cater to authors, students, other individuals and companies alike. With diverse imprints and a passion for effective usage of the English language, we're 'painting the world, one word at a time.' Let's connect and explore potential collaborations.

Go ahead and give yours a go:

_____
_____
_____
_____
_____
_____
_____
_____
_____
_____
_____
_____
_____
_____
_____
_____
_____
_____
_____

Step 3: Attend Networking Events

The day has come! It is time for you to attend your events; at least one of them. If they aren't close enough in the month, then come back to this section when you have attended the second one. Do ensure they both happen within 30 days.

Attend the selected networking events with a positive and open mindset. Be prepared to introduce yourself and your business using your elevator pitch. It is the first time, so I know it can be nerve racking, but be ready. Once you start talking to people at the event, it will become easier and you will be ready to tell everyone what you do when they ask.

At the event, engage in conversations, ask questions, and actively listen to others. Your task is to **speak with at least two people at each event**. No pressure, but after the event, fill in the table below. (Tip: Bring business cards with you and exchange with people who you think will make use of your contact information.)

Event 1 Event Name:	
Name two people you met at this event and write down at least one thing that you found interesting about each of them.	
Do you want to connect with anyone you met at the event? If so, why?	
What did you like most about the event that you attended?	

What didn't you like about the event?	
Would you attend the event again? Why?	
Event 2 **Event Name**:	
Name two people you met at this event and write down at least one thing that you found interesting about each of them.	
Do you want to connect with anyone you met at the event? If so, why?	
What did you like most about the event that you attended?	
What didn't you like about the event?	
Would you attend the event again? Why?	

Now, in terms of future events, what would you do differently? Write down anything you find useful.

For example, I attended a networking event where they invite different speakers to give a power session on different business topics each week. Each month, they list all the topics they will speak about that month and who the speaker will be for each topic. So, I looked at the areas I needed improvement on, researched the speakers, and marked off the sessions I wanted to attend.

Step 4: Connect with New Contacts

It's time to take action. Build your network.

After each of the two events, take time to follow up with at least two new connections you made. Send a personalized email or message expressing your interest in continuing the conversation or exploring potential collaborations. Offer to meet for a coffee or a virtual chat.

Do not wait for the following day. Send the message immediately and get it out of the way. This task should only take a few minutes.

Step 5: Nurture Relationships

This is the final step but it is ongoing. Building meaningful relationships takes time. Continuously nurture the connections you've made by staying in touch, sharing valuable content, and offering support when possible. Keep track of your interactions and set reminders for follow-ups. You do not have to ask them to help you with anything or offer any help immediately; the aim is not to just find something to ask for or give. However, you never know how this relationship will come in handy down the line. Someone you met at the event might not be someone who goes to the salon now, but you might be their go to when they are getting married three years later. They'll run to you to style their hair and their entire bridal party's.

Word of Advice

Networking is an ongoing process that can lead to valuable collaborations, partnerships, and opportunities for your business. Use this exercise as a starting point to expand your professional network and foster meaningful relationships. However, continuously network. I try to network at least once per month. Set a realistic networking goal for yourself and your business. If you have staff, they can get involved in networking as well.

Time Management and Productivity: Mastering Your Daily Tasks

"Time is a currency you can only spend once, so make sure you invest it wisely."

– Lisa Price

I have developed this workbook similarly to one of my courses and it feels the exact same as when an in-person course is coming to an end. Almost like I will be saying goodbye to you shortly and I'm unsure of when our paths will cross again... Okay, let me snap out of it.

Our next task is building effective time management skills, which is the key to productivity. In this exercise, you'll learn to prioritize tasks using the Eisenhower Box, create a daily to-do list, and harness the power of focused work intervals with the Pomodoro Technique. If you do not know what any of this means just yet, don't worry. By now you know that I'll walk you through it.

Step 1: The Eisenhower Box

The Eisenhower Box, also known as the Eisenhower Matrix, is a time management and productivity tool that helps with the prioritization of tasks based on their urgency and importance. This matrix was popularized by former U.S. President Dwight D. Eisenhower, who was known for his exceptional ability to manage his time and responsibilities effectively.

The Eisenhower Box consists of a simple grid divided into four quadrants, each representing a different category for tasks:

1. **Urgent and Important (Do First):** Tasks in this quadrant are both urgent and important, requiring your immediate attention. These are typically high-priority tasks that have significant consequences if not completed promptly. They should be tackled as soon as possible. For example, if your rent is due on

the first day of the month and it is the last day of the previous month, it is a Do First task. Not paying your rent poses a problem with your landlord, which can then affect your business.

2. **Important, but Not Urgent (Schedule):** Tasks in this quadrant are important but not time sensitive. They contribute to long-term goals, personal development, and overall productivity. It's advisable to schedule these tasks and allocate dedicated time to work on them regularly. I usually put most of my knowledge building activities in this quadrant. Oftentimes, I need to learn things to serve my business better but completing a course in six months can be on my *schedule*; it does not have to be *done right now*. Whether or not I complete the course will not necessarily put my business in jeopardy.

3. **Urgent, but Not Important (Delegate):** Tasks in this quadrant are urgent but not particularly important for you to handle personally. Delegating these tasks to others, if possible, can free up your time for more critical responsibilities. You do not have to be the one to send out an invoice or quote, for example, if you have a team.

4. **Not Urgent and Not Important (Eliminate):** Tasks in this quadrant are neither urgent nor important. They often represent distractions or time-wasting activities that can be eliminated or minimised to improve overall productivity. Avoid spending too much time on these tasks. Checking your company's social media every hour is neither important nor urgent.

Here's that example in the form of a matrix:

	URGENT	NOT URGENT
IMPORTANT	**Do First!** Edit and post today's blog post.	**Schedule** Spend an hour on Instagram responding to comments and DMs.
NOT IMPORTANT	**Delegate** Ask PA to call back client and schedule interview.	**Eliminate** Do not check Instagram every hour!

To use the Eisenhower Box effectively, follow these steps:

1. **List Your Tasks:** Start by listing all the tasks and activities you need to address, whether they are work-related, personal, or a combination of both.

2. **Categorize Tasks:** Place each task into one of the four quadrants based on its level of urgency and importance.

3. **Prioritize:** Focus your attention on tasks in the "Do First" quadrant. These are your top priorities and should be completed as soon as possible. Next, schedule tasks from the "Schedule" quadrant. Delegate tasks from the "Delegate" quadrant to appropriate individuals. Finally, consider eliminating tasks from the "Eliminate" quadrant, as they may not contribute significantly to your goals.

4. **Regular Review:** Continuously update and review your Eisenhower Box as new tasks emerge or priorities shift.

Go to the next page to complete the Eisenhower Box according to your own circumstances. List your daily tasks and projects. Assign each task to one of the four categories in your Eisenhower Box. Be honest and specific when categorizing.

	URGENT	NOT URGENT
IMPORTANT	Do First!	Schedule
NOT IMPORTANT	Delegate	Eliminate

Step 2: Daily To-Do List

From the Eisenhower Box you completed on the previous page, create a daily to-do list by selecting tasks from the "Urgent and Important" and "Important, but Not Urgent" categories. These are your top priorities for the day. Set a realistic number of tasks to ensure you can accomplish them.

This is a visual representation of which quadrants you will find these tasks in:

	URGENT	NOT URGENT
IMPORTANT	**Do First!**	**Schedule**

Now, create your daily to-do list using the space provided.

Monday

Tuesday

Wednesday

Thursday

Friday

Saturday

Sunday

Step 3: Pomodoro Technique

In all honesty, I am one of those people who procrastinate but get the job done regardless. I work well under pressure. Nevertheless, my health requires that I do not deal with the pressure at all or extremely infrequently. The Pomodoro Technique in combination with the Eisenhower Box makes quite the difference for me. I have utilised both, almost always together, in many different aspects of my life, from completing my degrees to running my businesses.

The Pomodoro Technique is a time management method developed by Francesco Cirillo in the late 1980s. It's a simple yet highly effective approach for improving both productivity and focus, especially when working on tasks that require concentration. Interestingly, the technique is named after the Italian word for 'tomato' because Cirillo initially used a tomato-shaped kitchen timer to track his work intervals.

Here's how the Pomodoro Technique works:

1. **Choose a Task:** Start by selecting a specific task or project that you want to work on. It's essential to choose something that can be broken down into smaller, manageable segments.

2. **Set a Timer:** Set a timer for a fixed period, traditionally 25 minutes. This time interval is known as a 'Pomodoro.' The Pomodoro Technique is built on the principle of focused, uninterrupted work for a short duration.

3. **Work Intensely:** During the Pomodoro, work on your chosen task with complete focus and dedication. Avoid any distractions, such as checking emails, social media, or unrelated tasks. I put my phones on silent and ensure everyone in my physical space knows I must not be disturbed.

4. **Complete the Pomodoro:** When the timer goes off after 25 minutes, stop working on the task, even if you're in the middle of something. This interruption is intentional and serves as a break point.

5. **Take a Short Break:** After completing a Pomodoro, take a short break of around 5 minutes. Use it for a toilet, tea, or water break, so you don't have to go in the next Pomodoro. Otherwise, use the time

to stretch, relax, or do something enjoyable but unrelated to work. Just don't take longer than the break allows.

6. **Repeat:** Return to the task and set the timer for another 25-minute Pomodoro. Continue this cycle — working for 25 minutes and then taking a 5-minute break — until you complete four Pomodoros.

7. **Longer Break:** After completing four Pomodoros (approximately two hours of focused work), take a more extended break of 15-30 minutes. This break allows you to recharge and refocus before starting the next set of Pomodoros.

Key principles and tips for using the Pomodoro Technique effectively:

- **Single Tasking:** Focus on <u>one task</u> during each Pomodoro. Multitasking is discouraged as it can reduce productivity.

- **Track Progress:** Keep a record of completed Pomodoros to monitor your productivity and identify areas for improvement.

- **Adjust Pomodoro Length:** Some people find that a 25-minute Pomodoro is ideal, while others may prefer shorter or longer intervals. Experiment to find what works best for you.

- **Stay Flexible:** I know I said to take your break wherever you are in the task earlier but if you're in a flow state and don't want to interrupt your work at the end of a Pomodoro, it's okay to extend the session. However, be mindful not to overwork yourself. I also suggest that you only start introducing more flexibility when you have mastered this technique to an extent.

- **Minimize Interruptions:** During a Pomodoro, silence notifications, close unnecessary tabs or apps, and inform colleagues or family members that you're in a focused work session.

Have a go at it now. Choose an important task from your to-do list that you have been putting off and work on it. Set a timer for 25 minutes (a 'Pomodoro') and start working on your task. When the timer rings, take a 5-minute break. Do this four times. After four Pomodoros, take a longer break of 15-30 minutes if you still haven't completed the task. Keep going until you complete the task and tick it off your to-do list.

Step 4: Review and Adjust

At the end of your workday, review your task list and evaluate your productivity. Did you get more done than you normally would?

_____

If not, what do you think you can improve on to get the most out of this technique? (Were there any interruptions of your Pomodoro? Could you have eliminated those interruptions?)

_____
_____
_____
_____
_____
_____
_____
_____

If you were successful and this process improved your productivity, celebrate completed tasks. Then reflect on any tasks that were not accomplished. Adjust your approach for the next day accordingly.

Which tasks will you be working on tomorrow and how will you be changing your approach for those specific tasks?

_____
_____
_____
_____
_____
_____
_____
_____
_____
_____

Word of Advice: Effective time management and productivity require discipline and practice. If you do not get it right the first few times, keep trying. Both these techniques can improve your workflow significantly and help you serve your business better.

That's it for this section of the workbook. Cheers to your trees bearing fruit! Nothing beats seeing the fruits of your labour. Congratulations on all your progress thus far. Well done on investing in yourself. Let's complete the final reflection and affirmation section in this workbook.

Reflection

1. Thinking about the financial health of your business and the goals you've set; how do you feel? Write down three words to describe these feelings below (they do not have to be positive; be honest):

   _____

   _____

   _____

2. Considering the insights gained from the market research activity and the customer persona development process, what did you find most useful?

   _____

   _____

   _____

3. With the connections you've made through networking and relationship building, note three positives thus far:

   _____

   _____

   _____

4. Write down three impacts that using the Pomodoro Technique and the Eisenhower Matrix have had on your workflow and/or business:

_____

_____

_____

Affirmation Statements:

1. I am nourishing the financial growth of my business with informed decisions.

2. My network is a source of strength, and my connections fuel my growth.

Reflect and Grow

Mentorship and Support Network

"Mentorship is the bridge between where you are and where you want to be. Don't be afraid to seek guidance from those who have walked the path before you."

– Ursula Burns

We have come to the very last section in this workbook and one exercise I do not think that the workbook would be complete without. As a mentor and someone who has been mentored, I find this to be one of the greatest investments you can make in yourself not just as a business owner but as a person.

The idea that those who are where we want to be can be helpful in our journey is not cliché. Mentorship and a strong support network can provide invaluable guidance and motivation in your entrepreneurial journey. It is often a paid service but if you choose the right mentor, it can turn out to be the best investment you've made in yourself. I want you to make that investment (financially and/or otherwise).

Thus, in this exercise, you'll identify potential mentors, reach out to them, and actively engage with an entrepreneurial support group or online community.

Step 1: Identify Potential Mentors

This is not a task that you can rush. It takes time, so allow yourself seven days to complete this task. Dedicate an hour to researching and identifying three potential mentors within your industry or related fields each day for seven consecutive days. Look for individuals who have achieved what you aspire to accomplish or have expertise that aligns with your goals.

There are MANY 'mentors' out there, so do not take this task lightly. If you are looking to pay for this service, compare prices and skills before adding possible mentors to your list. You do not want to find that you cannot afford the mentor you like the most or that they do not actually work with people in your field. As you conduct this research, complete the tables below (one for each of your TOP FIVE possibilities).

Mentor's Name: Mentor's Speciality: Mentorship Fees: Location and Availability: Experience and Track Record:

Mentor's Name: Mentor's Speciality: Mentorship Fees: Location and Availability: Experience and Track Record:

Mentor's Name: Mentor's Speciality: Mentorship Fees: Location and Availability: Experience and Track Record:

Mentor's Name:

Mentor's Speciality:

Mentorship Fees:

Location and Availability:

Experience and Track Record:

Mentor's Name:

Mentor's Speciality:

Mentorship Fees:

Location and Availability:

Experience and Track Record:

References and Testimonials:

Step 2: Reach Out for Mentorship

With your top five mentors' information on hand, it's time to craft a personalized message to each, explaining your goals, why you admire their work, and how you believe their guidance could benefit your journey. Be concise and respectful in your outreach. Again, do not procrastinate. Spend 45 minutes to an hour on this task.

Example of Mentorship Outreach:

Hello Leana,

I hope this message finds you well. I have been following your work in [industry/field] and have great admiration for your achievements, particularly in [mention specific accomplishments].

I'm in the early stages of setting up my business and believe your insights and guidance could be invaluable to me. I'm eager to learn and grow, and I would be honoured to have the opportunity to be mentored by you.

Thank you for considering my request. I look forward to reading your reply.

Warm regards,

[Your Name]

Please DO NOT copy this as it is. We don't want mentors all having the exact same email sent to them over the next few weeks from multiple people all across the globe! Not cute.

Here's your chance to write your own. Have a go at it:

_____
_____
_____
_____
_____
_____
_____

Step 3: Join an Entrepreneurial Support Group

I find this to be extremely useful. No matter what stage you are in your entrepreneurial journey, being part of a support group can be useful. Entrepreneurship can be a very lonely place and being part of these groups helps you to 'be around' likeminded people who often understand what you are going through at different stages in your business.

Research and identify an entrepreneurial support group, local organization, or online community that aligns with your business interests. Some are free and other charge fees based on the benefits. Choose based on your specific needs and depending on what's on offer. Look for groups that provide resources, networking opportunities, and peer support. Don't just find one for the sake of finding one.

Now, join one group. DO NOT join more than one just yet. Give yourself the chance to adjust to this new way of engaging with other entrepreneurs.

Step 4: Active Engagement

This is an ongoing part of the exercise. After joining the chosen support group or online community, actively participate by sharing your experiences, asking questions, and offering assistance to others. Engage in meaningful conversations, seek advice, and contribute to the community's growth. A group with silent members achieves absolutely nothing. If you find yourself in such group (wait for at least 10 days), leave and try out another one. Paid groups are often more engaging as the moderators have to deliver a paid service.

Step 5: Follow-Up with Potential Mentors

I haven't forgotten about your mentors! In this final task, you need to follow up. Have they gotten back to you? If so, who has and what have they said. If you don't receive a response within a reasonable time frame, say seven days, send a second email. Don't be discouraged; remember some emails go straight to spam. (I go through mine only once per week; others might too.) So, follow up and express your continued interest in connecting and learning from them.

For those who respond, proceed based on their responses. This is where you might need to schedule a call to see if you are the right fit.

NOTE: A mentor who does not assess you BEFORE agreeing to mentor you is one I would be weary of. Not every mentor is going to be the right fit for you and vice versa. An assessment must take place for your needs to be understood. Both of you must feel good about the possibility of working together.

If you are rejected by a mentor, ask for feedback. In the past, I have rejected someone for mentorship, given them feedback/homework, and then re-assessed them after a period of time before taking them on. If it is just a flat out no, also do not take it personally. Allow the universe to serve you. If it was meant to be, it would have been a yes.

In the same breath, do not be afraid to let a mentor know that you have changed your mind or that you do not think they would be the best fit for you. DO NOT SETTLE. This is your future and you get to decide how things go.

Keep looking until you find a mentor. There is someone out there to help you on your journey if that is what you want.

You did it!

Wow, we have come to the end of this workbook. You have completed all the exercises! Well done. I'm sending you a high-five and cheering for you from the sidelines. You deserve to win and I wish you nothing but the very best on your entrepreneurial journey moving forward.

Whatever you do, do not give up. Slow down if you have to, but you owe it to yourself to start that business or keep it going. You deserve to run a profitable business and you can do the work to make that possible.

Keep this book and go back to the different exercises when you need to, not just the ones that I advised you to. Continuously work on growing in your business and you will eventually be rewarded.

A year from now, I want you to go back through this book from start to finish and record your progress. I have created a *Great Entrepreneur in Training Journal*, which you can use then. Otherwise, get yourself any journal and use that. A year from now, if you have put in the work, you will be amazed at the progress you and your business have made.

Congratulations on everything you have done thus far! You've got this!

Build your accounting knowledge with the definitions I have left at the back of the workbook.

Self-Assessment Questionnaire

This is the same questionnaire as the one in the front of the book. Complete it in the same way you did before (hopefully, *a year ago*). You should notice a change in your score. It should be higher! That's progress. You can complete this as many times as you wish in the future, so always use a pencil. To differentiate and compare your progress, write down the date and score in pen somewhere on the last page of the questionnaire.

1) **How well do you understand your personal motivation and drive for entrepreneurship?**
   - 1 (Novice)
   - 2
   - 3
   - 4
   - 5 (Expert)

2) **How confident are you in articulating your business idea and its unique value proposition?**
   - 1 (Novice)
   - 2
   - 3
   - 4
   - 5 (Expert)

3) **How skilled are you in creating a vision board and mind map to define your business identity?**
   - 1 (Novice)
   - 2
   - 3
   - 4
   - 5 (Expert)

4) **How effectively can you assess your strengths and weaknesses for entrepreneurial success?**
   - 1 (Novice)
   - 2
   - 3
   - 4

- 5 (Expert)

5) **How proficient are you at setting SMART (Specific, Measurable, Achievable, Relevant, Time-bound) goals and action plans?**
   - 1 (Novice)
   - 2
   - 3
   - 4
   - 5 (Expert)

6) **How well can you evaluate the financial health and growth potential of your business?**
   - 1 (Novice)
   - 2
   - 3
   - 4
   - 5 (Expert)

7) **How skilled are you in conducting market research and developing customer personas?**
   - 1 (Novice)
   - 2
   - 3
   - 4
   - 5 (Expert)

8) **How confident are you in crafting a marketing and branding strategy for your business?**
   - 1 (Novice)
   - 2
   - 3
   - 4
   - 5 (Expert)

9) **How proficient are you at networking and building valuable relationships in your industry?**
   - 1 (Novice)
   - 2
   - 3
   - 4
   - 5 (Expert)

10) **How well can you manage your time and increase daily productivity?**
   - 1 (Novice)

- 2
- 3
- 4
- 5 (Expert)

11) **How experienced are you in seeking mentorship and establishing a support network for your entrepreneurial journey?**
- 1 (Novice)
- 2
- 3
- 4
- 5 (Expert)

12) **How knowledgeable are you about the legal requirements and regulations related to your business?**
- 1 (Novice)
- 2
- 3
- 4
- 5 (Expert)

13) **How skilled are you at creating and managing a budget for your business?**
- 1 (Novice)
- 2
- 3
- 4
- 5 (Expert)

14) **How effective are you at adapting to changes and pivoting your business strategy when needed?**
- 1 (Novice)
- 2
- 3
- 4
- 5 (Expert)

15) **How well can you assess market trends and identify emerging opportunities in your industry?**
- 1 (Novice)
- 2
- 3
- 4
- 5 (Expert)

16) **How skilled are you at creating and delivering persuasive pitches and presentations?**
   - 1 (Novice)
   - 2
   - 3
   - 4
   - 5 (Expert)

17) **How proficient are you at managing and optimizing your business finances, including cash flow and investments?**
   - 1 (Novice)
   - 2
   - 3
   - 4
   - 5 (Expert)

18) **How knowledgeable are you about intellectual property rights and protecting your business ideas?**
   - 1 (Novice)
   - 2
   - 3
   - 4
   - 5 (Expert)

19) **How experienced are you in building a strong online presence and leveraging digital marketing?**
   - 1 (Novice)
   - 2
   - 3
   - 4
   - 5 (Expert)

20) **How confident are you in handling negotiations and securing beneficial partnerships for your business?**
   - 1 (Novice)
   - 2
   - 3
   - 4
   - 5 (Expert)

21) **How well can you identify and address potential risks and challenges in your business plan?**
   - 1 (Novice)
   - 2

- 3
- 4
- 5 (Expert)

22) **How skilled are you at crafting compelling business proposals and securing funding or investment?**
   - 1 (Novice)
   - 2
   - 3
   - 4
   - 5 (Expert)

23) **How proficient are you at setting up and managing efficient business operations and logistics?**
   - 1 (Novice)
   - 2
   - 3
   - 4
   - 5 (Expert)

24) **How experienced are you in managing a team or outsourcing tasks effectively?**
   - 1 (Novice)
   - 2
   - 3
   - 4
   - 5 (Expert)

25) **How knowledgeable are you about customer service strategies and maintaining strong client relationships?**
   - 1 (Novice)
   - 2
   - 3
   - 4
   - 5 (Expert)

26) **How skilled are you at staying informed about industry trends and innovations?**
   - 1 (Novice)
   - 2
   - 3
   - 4
   - 5 (Expert)

27) **How proficient are you at evaluating the scalability and growth potential of your business model?**
- 1 (Novice)
- 2
- 3
- 4
- 5 (Expert)

28) **How effective are you at managing stress and maintaining a healthy work-life balance?**
- 1 (Novice)
- 2
- 3
- 4
- 5 (Expert)

29) **How confident are you in your ability to measure and analyse business performance using key metrics?**
- 1 (Novice)
- 2
- 3
- 4
- 5 (Expert)

30) **How proficient are you at adapting to emerging technologies and leveraging them for your business?**
- 1 (Novice)
- 2
- 3
- 4
- 5 (Expert)

31) **How knowledgeable are you about ethical and sustainable business practices?**
- 1 (Novice)
- 2
- 3
- 4
- 5 (Expert)

32) **How skilled are you at fostering a positive company culture and nurturing a motivated team?**
- 1 (Novice)
- 2

- 3
- 4
- 5 (Expert)

Calculate your score and see where you fall. Tick off both your score and its interpretation. Write the date here (_____).

Scoring Guidelines:

- Novice: 32 - 64
- Beginner: 65 - 96
- Intermediate: 97 - 128
- Advanced: 129 - 160
- Expert: 161 - 192

Interpreting Your Score:

- *Novice*: You have a lot to learn and explore in your entrepreneurial journey.
- *Beginner*: You have some knowledge but need to build your skills.
- *Intermediate*: You are making progress and have a good foundation.
- *Advanced*: You have a strong grasp of entrepreneurship but can continue to grow.
- *Expert*: You are highly skilled and experienced in entrepreneurship.

Additional Notes

Put it in Your Back Pocket

Accounting Terms Every Entrepreneur Must Know

1. **Assets:** Anything of value owned by the business, such as cash, accounts receivable, inventory, and property.

2. **Liabilities:** Financial obligations or debts that the business owes to creditors, suppliers, or lenders.

3. **Equity:** The owner's interest in the business, calculated as assets minus liabilities. It represents the net worth of the business.

4. **Revenue:** Income earned from sales of goods or services, also referred to as sales or turnover.

5. **Expenses:** Costs incurred to operate the business, including rent, utilities, salaries, and supplies.

6. **Gross Profit:** The difference between revenue and the cost of goods sold (COGS), representing the profitability of core business operations.

7. **Net Profit:** The profit remaining after deducting all expenses, including COGS, operating expenses, interest, and taxes.

8. **Cost of Goods Sold (COGS):** The direct costs associated with producing goods or services sold by the business.

9. **Balance Sheet:** A financial statement that provides a snapshot of a business's financial position, showing assets, liabilities, and equity at a specific point in time.

10. **Income Statement:** Also known as a profit and loss statement, it summarizes a business's revenue, expenses, and profit over a specified period.

11. **Cash Flow Statement:** A financial statement that tracks the movement of cash in and out of the business, categorizing it into operating, investing, and financing activities.

12. **Accounts Payable:** Money owed by the business to suppliers or creditors for goods or services purchased on credit.

13. **Accounts Receivable:** Money owed to the business by customers or clients for goods or services provided on credit.

14. **Depreciation:** The gradual decrease in the value of tangible assets, such as machinery or vehicles, over time.

15. **Accrual Accounting:** An accounting method that records revenue and expenses when they are earned or incurred, regardless of when cash is exchanged.

16. **Cash Accounting:** An accounting method that records revenue and expenses only when cash is received or paid.

17. **Financial Ratios:** Quantitative measures used to assess a business's financial performance and health, such as the current ratio, debt-to-equity ratio, and gross margin.

18. **Working Capital:** The difference between current assets and current liabilities, indicating a business's short-term liquidity.

19. **Earnings Before Interest and Taxes (EBIT):** A measure of a business's operating profit before interest and taxes are deducted.

20. **Break-Even Point:** The level of sales at which a business covers all its costs and neither makes a profit nor incurs a loss.

21. **Audit:** An independent examination of a business's financial statements and records by a qualified auditor to ensure accuracy and compliance with accounting standards.

22. **Amortization:** The gradual reduction of the value of intangible assets, such as patents or trademarks, over time.

23. **Dividends:** Distributions of profits to shareholders or business owners.

24. **Capital Expenditure (CapEx):** Spending on long-term assets, such as equipment or property, that are expected to provide future benefits.

25. **Operating Income:** The profit earned from core business operations, excluding interest and taxes.

26. **Retained Earnings:** Profits that are reinvested into the business rather than distributed to shareholders or owners.

27. **Trial Balance:** A list of all ledger accounts with their respective debit and credit balances to ensure that debits equal credits, verifying the accuracy of the accounting records.

About the Author

Kemone S-G Brown-Tshabalala is a dynamic entrepreneur, who excels in several key roles. As a writing coach and biographer/ghost-writer, Kemone works with individuals to turn their life stories into compelling narratives. In the business world, Kemone leverages her expertise to assist both profit and non-profit entrepreneurs in developing their ventures. Her portfolio includes launching over 30 successful businesses and aiding established companies in enhancing their communication through training and contractual communication services.

Kemone's dedication to mental health and well-being shines through her role as a workshop and retreat host, where she curates experiences tailored to improve the mental health of business owners and entrepreneurs. Her commitment to education and empowerment extends beyond borders. She passionately supports individuals in need and charitable organizations, particularly in her native Jamaica, by providing financial assistance as well as mentorship. With a profound love for research, writing, business, and making a positive impact, Kemone is officially a Publisher, Business Coach, Researcher, Biographer, Trainer, and International Keynote Speaker.

CONNECT WITH ME

Get the Book

Do you ever feel like your entrepreneurial journey is a solo trek up a steep mountain in very high heels?

Being a Black woman in the entrepreneurial world is no simple feat. The external challenges, coupled with the internal battles, can sometimes make the journey seem insurmountable.

This book isn't a compilation of idealized success stories. It's a genuine look into the lives of women who have been where you are right now. Women who've faced those very challenges, grappled with the self-doubt, and broken through the barriers meant to hold them back.

Read their stories: Raw, honest accounts of their journeys, packed with trials, tribulations, and so many triumphs.

Connect: Understand the shared experiences, the silent struggles, and the milestones that may mirror your own.

And for those looking for actionable insights and ways to develop as entrepreneurs in their own rights? **I have specially created a companion workbook to guide you on your own entrepreneurial path** (*Great Entrepreneur in Training*).

If you're seeking a genuine connection, understanding, and motivation, this book is for you.

Join this community and draw strength from shared experiences. Let's venture this challenging landscape of entrepreneurship together.

This book isn't just about entrepreneurial tales-it's a mosaic of life experiences, challenges faced, and victories celebrated. It's about finding your voice amidst the noise and discovering that you're not alone.

What You'll Discover Inside the Book:

- Personal accounts of confronting and conquering challenges in business and life.

- Lessons on how women overcome hurdles meant to derail their entrepreneurial journeys.

- Intimate reflections on growth during their entrepreneurial journey.

- Insights into navigating a business environment often dominated by different narratives.

After turning the last page, you'll:

- Feel inspired and empowered to overcome any challenges thrown your way.

- Be equipped with new perspectives and lessons for your own entrepreneurial journey.

- Understand the importance of support and the will to NEVER give up in business.

- Rekindle or discover your passion and drive to make your dreams a reality.

- Realize that your story, however unique, has a place in the world of business.

This book is ideal for:

- Aspiring Black women entrepreneurs seeking guidance and inspiration.

- Current business owners in need of reassurance and a fresh perspective.

- Anyone looking to understand and appreciate the diverse narratives of entrepreneurship.

- Supporters and allies wanting to elevate Black women's voices in business.

- Readers hungry for authentic, empowering stories that resonate.

Entrepreneurship is a journey filled with ups and downs. Every story in this book is a testament to the strength, resilience, and brilliance of Black women who've paved their own paths. Their words aren't just lessons; they're lifelines to anyone seeking to make their mark...

Don't just dream. Dare. Dive into these empowering narratives and let them fuel your journey.

SCAN HERE TO ORDER YOUR COPY

www.ingramcontent.com/pod-product-compliance
Lightning Source LLC
Chambersburg PA
CBHW041912190326
41458CB00023B/6245